mighty
MAC

mighty MAC

Airlift, Rescue, Special Operations

**René J Francillon, Peter B Lewis
& Jim Dunn**

OSPREY
AEROSPACE

Published in 1990 by Osprey Publishing Limited
59 Grosvenor Street, London W1X 9DA

© René J Francillon, Peter B Lewis & Jim Dunn

British Library Cataloguing in Publication Data

Françillon, René J. (Rene Jacques) 1937–
   Mighty Mac – (Colour series).
   1. United States. Air Force.
   Military aircraft. Camouflage &
   markings, history
I. Title   II. Lewis, Peter B.
358.4183

ISBN 0 85045 985 0

Editor Dennis Baldry
Page design by David Tarbutt
Printed in Hong Kong

Front cover *Coach 12*, a C-130E of the 115th Tactical Airlift Squadron, 146th Tactical Airlift Wing, California Air National Guard, over Santa Cruz Island off the coast of Southern California on 31 August 1989. Currently, 25 ANG squadrons are MAC-gained units

Title pages Ever since 1 December 1974, when the tactical airlift resources were transferred from TAC to MAC, and 31 March 1975, when those from the AAC, PACAF, and USAFE were added to MAC, the Herk folks have felt left out in the midst of MAC's heavy lifters and have expressed their frustration by calling themselves 'Little MAC.' Some have gone as far as wearing an appropriately sized 'Little MAC' patch underneath the standard MAC chest patch . . .

MSgt William A Weber, a loadmaster from the 115th TAS, CA ANG, on the open aft ramp of a C-130E during a flight over the Southern California coast on 31 August 1989

For a catalogue of all books published by Osprey Aerospace
please write to:

**The Marketing Manager, Consumer Catalogue Department
Osprey Publishing Ltd, 59 Grosvenor Street, London, W1X 9DA**

Introduction

Headquartered at Scott AFB, Illinois, the Military Airlift Command is proudly called 'The Backbone of Deterrence'. It possesses more than 1000 aircraft and has a personnel strength of over 94,000 active duty people, both military and civilian. It exercises direct command over 13 bases in the United States and controls US facilities at Lajes Field in the Azores and Rhein-Main AB in West Germany. Upon mobilization of Air Force Reserve (AFRES) and Air National Guard (ANG) forces, MAC will gain an additional 63,000 people and approximately 390 aircraft. Moreover, MAC's assets are supplemented in peacetime by those of commercial air carriers operating under military contracts and in time of emergency by those of carriers participating in the Civil Reserve Air Fleet (CRAF) programme.

MAC flying units are distributed among three numbered Air Forces. The Twenty-First Air Force, headquartered at McGuire AFB, New Jersey, has 11 Military Airlift Squadrons (two with C-5A/Bs, six with C-141Bs, one with C-22As and C-130Es, one with C-23As, and one with a mix of light transports and helicopters), four Tactical Airlift Squadrons with C-130Es, one Aeromedical Airlift Squadron with C-9As, and one Air Base Squadron with C-12s and C-21s. It also has jurisdiction over the prestigious 89th Military Airlift Wing at Andrews AFB, Maryland, which provides transportation for the President, the Vice President, cabinet members, top government officials, and foreign dignitaries. The Twenty-Second Air Force, with headquarters at Travis AFB, California, has 12 Military Airlift Squadrons (three with C-5A/Bs, eight with C-141Bs, and one with C-12s and C-21s), nine Tactical Airlift Squadrons with C-130E/Hs, and one Aeromedical Airlift Squadron with C-9As.

The Twenty-Third Air Force, headquartered at Hurlburt Field, Florida, conducts special operations as its primary mission. Its other missions include combat rescue, peacetime rescue coordination, security support for intercontinental ballistic missile sites, aeromedical evacuation, facility flight check operations, weather reconnaissance, and aerial sampling. Its six wings operate some 350 aircraft including AC-130/MC-130/HC-130 Hercules, four types of helicopters, C-9As, C-12A/Fs, and C-21As.

There are two basic types of AFRES airlift units. Eighteen Reserve Associate squadrons are located at MAC bases and share C-5A/Bs, C-9As and C-141Bs with active duty units. Twenty-two Reserve squadrons, which have their own aircraft, are tenant units at bases controlled by other Commands or are located at AFRES or ANG facilities. They include two MASs with C-5As, one MAS with C-141Bs, 13 TASs with C-130s, one SOS with AC-130As, one SOS with CH/HH-3Es, three ARRSs with HC-130s and helicopters, and one WRS with WC-130s. MAC-gained ANG units in 19 states include one MAS with C-5As, one MAS with C-141Bs, one SOS with EC-130Es, two ARRSs with HC-130s and HH-3s, and 20 TASs with C-130s.

Photographs for this Osprey book were gathered over a period of more than 20 years, with the more recent photographs being specially taken during visits to Altus AFB, Kirtland AFB, Pope AFB, Travis AFB, Schoonover Field, and Channel Islands ANGB. We are most grateful to our hosts at these bases and to the MAC/PAM staff at Scott AFB for their support. Special thanks to TSgt Kit Thompson and Lt Doug Kinneard for providing photo coverage of the 1st SOW and to our California Guard friends for their warm hospitality.

René J Francillon, Peter B Lewis, & Jim Dunn
Vallejo, California, January 1990

Additional photography by Tom Ackery, Christian Jacquet-Francillon, Toyokazu Matsuzaki, Paul Minert, and the United States Air Force.

Contents

With the Chugach Mountains as a backdrop, 69-5802, a Sikorsky HH-3E of the 71st Aerospace Rescue and Recovery Squadron, hovers at Elmendorf AFB, Alaska, in May 1984 (*Edric G Francillon*)

From MATS to MAC

Below The Military Airlift Command came into being on 1 January 1966 when the Military Air Transport Service was redesignated. The 375th Aeromedical Airlift Wing was activated on 12 January 1966, thus becoming the first new MAC unit. Its initial equipment consisted of Douglas MC-118As and Convair MC-131As fitted to transport patients between various medical facilities and military hospitals in the United States and abroad. Aircraft 51-3825 was photographed at Travis AFB, the site of the David Grant USAF Medical Center, on 30 April 1966

The Military Airlift Command retired its last two Douglas C-54 Skymasters in 1972. This C-54G-5-DO was assigned to the Commanding General, Fourth Air Force, Air Force Reserve, at McClellan AFB where it was photographed on 28 October 1967. The Fourth Air Force already controlled many of the reserve airlift squadrons

Rara avis: A Douglas RC-118A of the 1370th Photo Mapping Wing at Forbes AFB, Kansas, on 6 July 1968

VC-118A (53-3234) at Pago Pago,
American Samoa, October 1971
(*H L James*)

53-0330 of the 109th Military Airlift Squadron, Minnesota ANG, at the Minneapolis-St Paul Airport on 14 July 1968. This was one of the 135 Boeing KC-97G tankers converted as pure transports, with the refuelling boom and boomer station removed

Below Built as a C-119C and brought up to C-119G standard before being assigned to the 129th Air Commando Squadron, California ANG, this Flying Boxcar was photographed at McClellan AFB in April 1967. Redesignated 129th ARRS in May 1975, this MAC-gained unit is now equipped with Lockheed HC-130Ns and Ps and Sikorsky HH-3Es

Overleaf An MC-131A of the 375th Aeromedical Airlift Wing on the transient aircraft ramp at NAS Miramar, California, on 26 August 1967

Retrofitted with APS-42 radar in the nose and combustion heaters in wing-tip fairing, this Douglas C-124A of the 442nd Military Airlift Wing still bore Continental Air Command tail markings when seen at the Minneapolis-St. Paul Airport on 14 July 1968. No longer MAC-gained, this reserve unit from Richards-Gebaur AFB, Missouri, is now designated 442nd TFW and possesses two squadrons of A-10As, the 45th TFS at Grissom AFB, Indiana, and the 303rd TFS at Richards-Gebaur

Also belonging to the 304th ARRS and photographed on the same date (20 July 1968) as the preceding HU-16B, this Albatross is finished in the camouflage scheme adopted for combat rescue operations during the Southeast Asia War

Grumman Albatross amphibians were operated by active units from the Air Rescue Service (redesignated Aerospace Rescue and Recovery Service in January 1966 when MAC replaced MATS) between 1949 and 1967. HU-16Bs remained in service with AFRES units for six more years (including with the 304th ARRS in Portland, Oregon, to which this aircraft belonged)

Below C-133B (59-0524) of the 60th MAW at McClellan AFB, 12 September 1966. Notwithstanding difficulties with their Pratt & Whitney T34 propeller-turbines and fatigue problems, Douglas C-133 Cargomasters equipped three squadrons for ten years before being withdrawn from use in 1971 following the entry into service of the Lockheed C-5A. The last two C-133As and the 15 C-133Bs were fitted with clamshell rear-loading doors which enabled them to carry fully assembled Atlas ICBMs and Thor and Jupiter IRBMs

Right Convair VT-29D used as a staff transport by the 60th MAW, Travis AFB, 17 May 1969

Bottom right Two and one half years after MAC had been organized many of its aircraft, such as this C-133B of the 60th MAW at Travis AFB, still showed clearly where the words Military Air Transport Service had been overpainted to display the new Military Airlift Command title

Following spread Equipped with C-124 Globemaster IIs, the 336th Military Airlift Squadron also possessed this smart-looking Cessna U-3A. This AFRES squadron was based at Hamilton AFB, California, where this photograph was taken on 21 May 1971

The *City of Torrington*, a Lockheed
C-121G of the 187th Military Airlift
Squadron, Wyoming ANG, at the
Cheyenne Municipal Airport on 28
June 1971

Based at the Savannah Municipal Airport, the 158th Military Airlift Squadron, 165th Military Airlift Group, Georgia ANG, flew C-124Cs between 1967 and 1974. This aircraft was photographed at McClellan AFB in August 1973, 13 months before the unit was redesignated 158th TAS/165th TAG and re-equipped with Lockheed C-130Es

Taken at NAS Alameda, California, on 24 September 1971, this photograph of a C-124A of the AFRES presents an historical puzzle. The designation of the unit is clearly painted as 452nd MAW on the nosewheel door. Yet, at that time this wing was still officially designated 452nd Troop Carrier Wing, Medium. It was redesignated 452nd Military Airlift Wing on 1 April 1972, six months after this photograph had been taken

On 1 December, 1974, the Air Force
directed the transfer of tactical airlift
resources from TAC to MAC. At the
same time tactical squadrons of the
reserve forces (AFRES and ANG)
became MAC-gained units. This
C-7A of the MAC-gained 300th
TAS, 94th TAW, AFRES, was
photographed at Travis AFB in July
1977

A Fairchild UC-123K of the 355th
Tactical Airlift Squadron, 302nd
Tactical Airlift Wing, AFRES, in
transit at Travis AFB in July 1977.
This reserve wing was then based at
Rickenbacker AFB, Ohio

Little MAC

A C-130A Hercules (56-0537) from the 64th TAS, AFRES, making an assault landing on a dirt strip at Fort Bragg, North Carolina, during the *Airlift Rodeo* competition in June 1983 (*Paul Minert*)

C-130A (56-0497) of the
MAC-gained 142nd TAS, Delaware
ANG, landing at McClellan AFB on
21 November 1981

Right An enthusiastic crew chief
from the 156th TAS, North Carolina
ANG, got carried away with the
dayglo paint during a 1987 training
exercise for MAC-gained forestry
fire-fighting units from the Air Force
Reserve and the Air National Guard

Military Airlift Command was late getting into the jet age as budgetary constraints initially prevented it from acquiring anything more than 15 Boeing C-135Bs. Although the Hercules had been designed as a tactical transport, shortage of jet- or turbine-powered aircraft forced MAC to order C-130Es for strategic airlift missions. This C-130E from the 438th MAW, a unit based at McGuire AFB, New Jersey, was photographed in Peoria, Illinois, on 13 May 1967

Below Ski-equipped C-130D of the 17th Tactical Airlift Squadron, 21st Composite Wing, from Elmendorf AFB, Alaska. In this instance, high-visibility arctic markings and skis appear quite out of place as the aircraft is taxying at McClellan AFB, a California base from which snow is conspicuously missing, on 9 November 1972

Right Desert camouflage was applied to a small number of C-130Es, particularly those assigned to the 435th Tactical Airlift Wing, a MAC unit based at Rhein-Main AB in Germany to support USAFE operations in Europe and the Middle East. Unfortunately, this created scheduling problems as aircraft in desert camouflage were often flying over dark forests in Central Europe while dark camouflaged C-130Es stood like sore thumbs over the desert (*Tom Akery*)

Bottom right C-130E (70-1273) of the 317th TAW at Travis AFB, 26 September 1976

Held at Pope AFB, North Carolina, in early June, *Airlift Rodeo '89* was plagued by unusually heavy rainfalls. Hence, the assault landing event could not be held on dirt strips at Fort Bragg but had to take place on a paved runway at Pope AFB

Left Every afternoon the attention of *Airlift Rodeo* participants is focused on the posting of results . . .

Top right 'The Air Force puts us to sleep . . .' Paratroopers of the 82nd Airborne Division catch a few winks while awaiting to board a C-130E of the 317th Tactical Airlift Wing at Pope AFB

Right As a former airport design engineer, the photographer was not surprised by the size of the drainage ditch over which this C-130E of the 317th TAW is taxying. When it rains at Pope AFB it really pours!

Above Golden hills, coastal fog, blue sea, bright sky. This is California! A C-130E of the 146th TAW, California ANG, hugs the hills on Santa Cruz Island during a flight from its nearby home base, Channel Islands ANGB on the edge of NAS Point Mugu in Port Hueneme

Right During the summer and early fall, aircrews from the 115th TAS, 146th TAW, California ANG, have ample opportunity to practice contour flying in mountainous terrain as they train for forest-fire fighting and are called to fight fires up and down western states

Smile! You are on candid camera. Lt Col Clyde Doheney and Capt Nick Daffern bring *Coach 12* close to the open aft ramp of *Coach 11* during a memorable flight with the 115th TAS, 146th TAW, California ANG, on 31 August 1989. The photographer had some difficulties avoiding the glare from the left seat in *Coach 12*!

Just let us enter the race and we'll show these Unlimited folks what low flying is all about! A C-130E of the 115th TAS, 146th TAW, California ANG, flies by during the 1989 Reno Air Races

Left Operations from dirt fields are regularly practiced by active and reserve Herk crews. This C-130E of the 314th TAW, a MAC wing from Little Rock AFB, Arkansas, does it in the California dirt at Schoonover Field on the Fort Hunter Liggett Military Reservation on 11 September 1989

Bottom Left *Airlift Rodeo '83*: A C-130H of the MAC-gained 185th TAS, Oklahoma ANG, making an assault landing at the Sicily Drop Zone, Fort Bragg, North Carolina—a US Army base featured in the Osprey *Superbase* series (*Paul Minert*)

Below The C-130Hs of the 21st TAS, 374th TAW, unlike the C-130Es of this unit based at Clark AB in the Philippines, are painted light grey overall and only carry small (quickly painted over?) national insignia. Aircraft 73-1580 was photographed on 12 August 1989 while on final approach to Yokota AB, Japan (*Toyokazu Matsuzaki*)

Right C-130E (63-7765) of the 314th TAW taking off at Schoonover Field, Fort Hunter Liggett Military Reservation, on 11 September 1989

Below C-130E of the 115th TAS, 146th TAW, California ANG, during a low-altitude container drop near Palmdale, California, 30 August 1989

Well-known in Europe, but not yet seen in the United States, Short C-23A Sherpas of the 10th Military Airlift Squadron, a MAC unit based at Zweibrücken AB, Germany, fulfill a vital role by transporting spare parts between depots and operational USAFE bases (*Courtesy of Christian Jacquet-Francillon*)

Pending the selection and acquisition of a small turboprop-powered transport aircraft, which will be designated C-27A, the Military Airlift Command is leasing some CASA 212s from Evergreen International for use by the Southern Command at Howard AFB in the Canal Zone. This CASA 212, complete with US military insignia and Air Force serial number, was photographed on 9 June 1989 at Pope AFB, North Carolina, where Air Force crews were being trained on the Spanish-built aircraft

Weight Lifters

After entering service in April 1965, Lockheed C-141As were left in natural metal finish for several years as shown by this StarLifter of the 60th MAW at Travis AFB on 25 August 1968. StarLifters played a vital role during the Southeast Asia War primarily by operating over an 'air bridge' between Aerial Ports of Embarkation in the United States and operating bases in South Vietnam, the Philippines, Guam, and Thailand. They also flew over 6000 aeromedical evacuation sorties. Above all, however, they will always be remembered for being the primary aircraft during *Operation Homecoming*, the repatriation of POWs from North Vietnam in 1973

Inset Bearing the badges of the 438th MAW, Military Arilift Command, and the 514th MAW (Associate), AFRES, the two wings sharing C-141Bs at McGuire AFB, New Jersey, this StarLifter was ready to depart from Point Saline Airport, Grenada's infamous Cuban-built airport, on 5 September 1984

U

C. STATE FORCE C-141
AF SERIAL NO.: 650088
SERVICE THIS A/C WITH
GRADE JP-4 FUEL
R.F.T.O.42131-1-14

THE
Golden Bear
8088
60TH MAW

Named *Golden Bear*, the Ursidae species which is California's mascot, this C-141B (63-8088) is assigned to the 60th MAW at Travis AFB. Since these two photographs were taken on 21 August 1982, the aircraft has been repainted in the now standard (but, oh so unattractive) dark camouflage scheme

Bearing the badge of the 443rd
Military Airlift Wing (Training) from
Altus AFB, Oklahoma, this C-141A
was photographed at NAS Fallon,
Nevada, on 28 September 1976

Since its 36th TAS was inactivated in the fall of 1989, the 62nd MAW at McChord AFB, Washington, only has two squadrons of C-141Bs, the 4th and 8th Military Airlift Squadrons

Left Making a tactical approach instead of the more usual long and flat approach favoured for most airlift operations, this C-141B clearly shows the dorsal hump housing its air refuelling receptacle

Bottom left A C-141A StarLifter of the 60th MAW landing at McClellan AFB on 23 August 1971

Below As a violent storm was approaching Altus AFB, Oklahoma, in the afternoon of 2 May 1989, the 443rd Military Airlift Wing (Training), the wing responsible for training C-141B and C-5 crews, kept up its activities. The next morning flying operations were markedly less intense . . .

The tenth *Airlift Rodeo* was held at Pope AFB from 5 through 9 June 1989. Participants included 15 MAC units (two with C-5Bs, five with C-141Bs, seven with C-130E/Hs, and one with MC-130E), 10 AFRES units (four with C-141Bs and six with C-130B/E/Hs), six ANG units with C-130A/B/Hs, one Marine Corps reserve unit with KC-130Ts, and six foreign units (four with C-130Hs/ CC-130Hs/Hercules C. 1Ps and two with C. 160 Transalls)

Before departing Pope AFB at the end of the *Airlift Rodeo* competition, the participants often apply temporary—and totally non-reg—markings and proudly fly their unit's standard as does this C-141B from the 63rd MAW seen on its way back to Norton AFB, California

HI, JEANIE
BONNIE
SARA
JEFF
LORENZO
DON'T PAINT
KATHY
HI.
LINDA
HAL
ASHLEY
RHODA
FREDDY
LOVES
CATHY
BUCKWHEAT

Soldier, you are out of uniform! A C-141B from the 315th MAW departing Pope AFB at the end of *Airlift Rodeo '89*. Had there been a 'zapping' contest, this would have had to be the winner

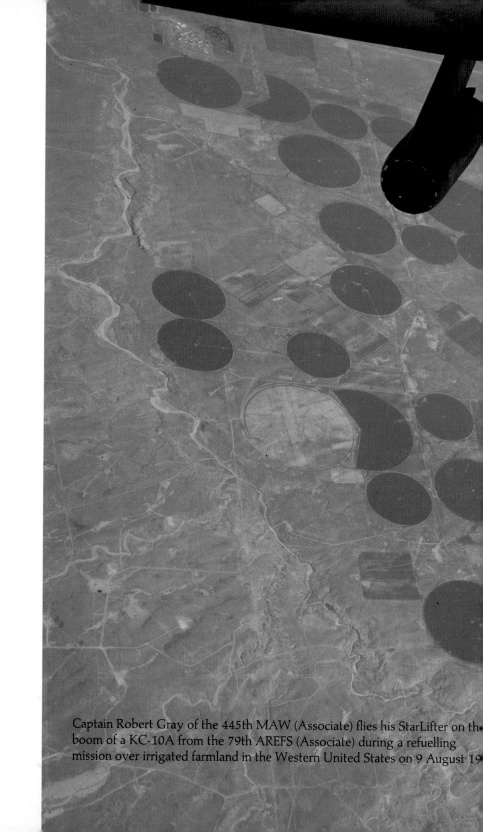

Captain Robert Gray of the 445th MAW (Associate) flies his StarLifter on the
boom of a KC-10A from the 79th AREFS (Associate) during a refuelling
mission over irrigated farmland in the Western United States on 9 August 19

Right On the occasion of *Airlift Rodeo '89*, a C-5B of the 436th MAW (aircraft 86-0017) set a new world record by airdropping a 193,550-lb load consisting of four Sheridan tanks and 73 paratroopers. Lockheed did not miss this publicity opportunity and provided the troopers with a special helmet badge. Now that the C-5As have been re-winged and as the C-5Bs were fitted with the strengthened wings during construction, all Galaxies operated by two MAC wings (the 60th and 436th MAWs), two AFRES associate wings (the 349th and 512th MAWs), two AFRES squadron (the 68th MAS and 337th MAS, 433rd MAW), and one ANG squadron (the 137th MAS, 105th MAG, NY ANG) are fully mission-capable

Bottom right A C-5A of the 60th MAW taxying at Travis AFB in the afternoon of 2 July 1981. The KC-135As barely visible in the background belonged to the 307th Air Refueling Group, a SAC tenant unit which was inactivated two years later

Below StarLifter on final approach to Runway 21R at Nellis AFB on 21 August 1987

Having just flown over the Golden
Gate Bridge on the western edge of
San Francisco Bay, a Travis-based
C-5A is on his way across the Pacific
(*USAF*)

Left A young crew chief from the 443rd MAW (Training) at Altus AFB remains in contact with the flight crew as her C-5A is about to leave the ramp on 2 May 1989

Below C-5B giving its best Darth Vader imitation

Right When the McClellan Air Museum needed a Grumman Albatross to be transported from Luke AFB, its call for help was answered by the reservists of the 433rd MAW. The C-5A disgorging the Albatross is aircraft 70-0445. Although it arrived at McClellan AFB in USAF markings on 25 March 1988, the Albatross had last been operated by the Coast Guard as an HU-16E (USCG 7209); it had been built as an SA-16A (51-7209) for the Air Force

MILITARY AIRLIFT COMMAND

Main picture Night maintenance work at Travis AFB on 22 May 1989. The C-5A shared by the 60th MAW and 349th MAW (Associate) will soon be back up in the air. However, the wingless C-141B, which had been heavily damaged in a ground accident, will remain grounded for several months

Below Night view of the cavernous main deck of the C-5B

Dusk comes to the crowded ramp at Travis AFB. The active MAC wing, the 60th MAW, and its AFRES associate unit, the 349th MAW, share 36 C-5A/Bs and an equal number of C-141Bs

Weather, Mapping & Aeromedevac

Main picture The first of 34 WB-47Es modified from B-47E bombers was delivered to the Air Weather Service, Military Air Transport Service, on 20 March 1963. The last was sent to MASDC (Military Aircraft Storage & Disposition Center) at Davis-Monthan AFB on 31 October 1969. Note the air sampling equipment beneath the centre fuselage of this aircraft from the 55th Weather Reconnaissance Squadron taxying at McClellan AFB on 22 May 1967

Inset A Boeing WB-47E of the 55th Weather Reconnaissance Squadron at McClellan AFB on 28 January 1968. The weather birds were the last Stratojets in Air Force service

The Air Weather Service received the first of 19 WB-57Fs on 18 June 1964 and assigned them to the 58th Weather Reconnaissance Squadron at Kirtland AFB, New Mexico, for use in the high-altitude aerial sampling mission. The last WB-57Fs were phased out when the 58th WRS was inactivated on 1 July 1974. Aircraft 63-13298, which had been built by Martin as a B-57B with the serial 52-1536 and was later rebuilt as an RB-57F by General Dynamics, was photographed at McClellan AFB on 17 March 1968

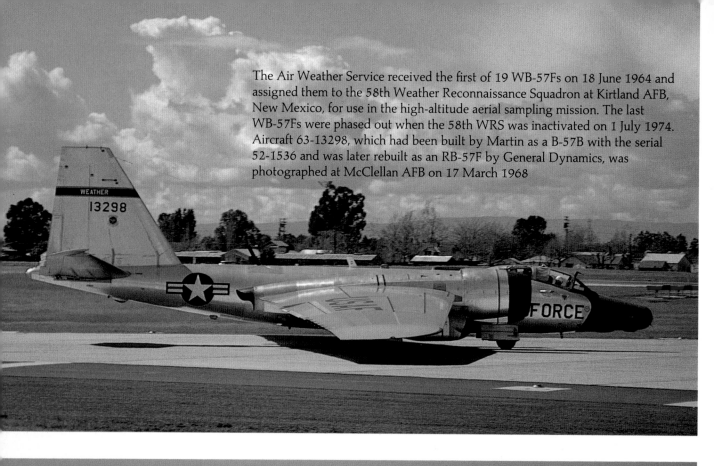

In addition to WB-57Fs, the 58th WRS flew WB-57Cs, including 53-3851 seen at McClellan AFB on 22 April 1972 with sampling equipment in modified tip tanks. At peak strength in 1962, two years before receiving its WB-57Fs, the Air Weather Service had 38 WB-57s

Right Delivered by Lockheed as an HC-130H, 65-0972 was later modified as a WC-130H. The WC-130Bs have been phased out and, for budgetary reasons, WC-130Es and WC-130Hs have now been assigned to a single AFRES squadron, the 815th WRS, at Keesler AFB

Below For flying in and around hurricanes and typhoons the Air Weather Service first received five WC-130Bs in 1962 and later acquired 11 more WC-130Bs as well as six WC-130Es and 15 WC-130Hs. This WC-130E of the 53rd Weather Reconnaissance Squadron based at Keesler AFB, Mississippi, was detached to Andersen AFB on Guam where it was photographed on 22 October 1982

Top Ten C-135Bs were modified as WC-135Bs to replace WB-47E low-to-medium altitude weather reconnaissance aircraft. Entering service in 1965, the WC-135Bs were initially shared by the 55th WRS at McClellan AFB, where 61-2674 was photographed on 22 October 1976, and the 56th WRS at Yokota AB, Japan

Above MATS had been given control of the Air Photographic and Charting Service on 16 April 1952. APCS was re-organized as the 1370th Photo Mapping Group on 5 April 1954, redesignated 1370th Photo Mapping Wing on 1 January 1960, and inactivated on 30 June 1972. Four Boeing RC-135As, including 63-8058 seen at Forbes AFB on 6 July 1968, were operated by the 1371st MCS, 1370th PMW, beginning in 1965

Right With a coat of paint over its original natural metal finish, 61-2674 is seen on take-off at McClellan AFB on 1 February 1982. The cylindrical object on the side of the centre fuselage is an U-1 foil collector. Another one is located on the port side

83

To photograph Space Shuttle launch and recovery activities, as well as other classified projects, several WC-135Bs have been fitted with a *Star Cast* electro-optical system. Distinguishing features include the addition of two optical windows in the main deck cargo door on the port side of the forward fuselage. Landing at McClellan AFB on 5 January 1990, 61-2672 displays the new scheme recently adopted for the WC-135B fleet

Following successful evaluation of the RC-130A prototype, Lockheed delivered 15 new aircraft in the RC-130A configuration. They were assigned by MATS and then by MAC to the 1375th MCS, 1370th PMW

Left Aircraft 54-1632, the 19th C-130A, was first modified as a TC-130A trainer and later as the prototype for the RC-130A photo-mapping version. As an RC-130A it served with the 1375th Mapping and Charting Squadron, 1370th Photo Mapping Wing, first at Turner AFB, Georgia, and then at Forbes AFB, Kansas. This roman nose prototype was photographed at the latter on 6 July 1968

Below After overnighting at Travis AFB, a C-9A of the 11th AAS, 375th AAW, departs in the morning of 23 May 1989 for a flight to Norton AFB in California, Luke AFB and Davis-Monthan AFB in Arizona, Biggs AFB in Texas, and finally back to its home base at Scott AFB in Illinois. In a typical year, C-9As (supplemented as required by C-130s and C-141s temporarily fitted with litters) carry 80,000 patients on 2350 aeromedical evacuation missions. Most of the C-9As are operated by the 11th Aeromedical Airlift Squadron, 375th Aeromedical Airlift Wing, on a domestic network centred on Scott AFB, Illinois. In addition, three are with the 20th AAS at Clark AB in the Philippines and five are with the 55th AAS at Rhein-Main AB in Germany

Right SRA Chris A Bohls, a Medical Technician from the 57th Aeromedical Evacuation Squadron, supervising the boarding of military passengers in a C-9A of the 375th AAW at Travis AFB

VIP & Liaison

C-21A (40128) of the 1400th MAS at Norton AFB in November 1986 (*Paul Minert*)

Below CT-39A (62-4488) of the
1400th MAS Det 1 at McClellan AFB
in December 1976

Right A Gates Learjet C-21A, a
Beech C-12F, and a North American
CT-39A of the 1400th Military
Airlift Squadron at Norton AFB,
California, in March 1986 shortly
before the last CT-39s were retired
(*Paul Minert*)

Left Except for its radio call number on the fin, this Gulfstream C-20B carried no military markings when photographed at Pope AFB where it had brought General Duane H Cassidy, CINCMAC, for *Airlift Rodeo '89*

Bottom left Now retired, Lockheed VC-140Bs had been part of the Special Airlift Mission (SAM) fleet of the 89th MAW at Andrews AFB since 1961. This VC-140A was photographed at NAS Miramar on 9 August 1974

Below Also wearing the distinctive paint scheme applied to SAM aircraft, this VC-131H had taken senior Air National Guard officers to Tyndall AFB on the occasion of *William Tell '78*

The VC-9C which brought General Duane H Cassidy, CINCMAC, to McClellan AFB on 8 August 1989, shortly before his retirement. on the occasion of the activation of the new headquarters for the Air Rescue Service. Previously, this headquarters had been located at Scott AFB

Above One of the three C-137Bs of the 89th MAW

Right A Boeing C-135B (62-4130) of the 89th MAW landing at Yokota AB, Japan, on 24 July 1989 (*Toyokazu Matsuzaki*)

Bottom left After serving as a standard utility helicopter with the 40th Aerospace Rescue and Recovery Squadron, Det 6, at Holloman AFB, New Mexico, this UH-1N underwent depot maintenance and came out in a smart new VIP scheme. In 1989, it was assigned to the 58th Military Airlift Squadron at Ramstein AB, Germany

No book on MAC would be complete without a photograph of Air Force One.
Here it is landing at the San Jose Municipal Airport where it was bringing
President Gerald Ford during his unsuccessful presidential campaign in 1976

Rescue & Special Ops

Below Twenty HC-130Ps were built for the Aerospace Rescue and Recovery Service. Aircraft 66-0211, at McClellan AFB on 11 September 1968, wears the standard camouflage applied for combat rescue operations in Southeast Asia

Top right An HC-130H (65-0973) of the 41st ARRS at McClellan on 21 May 1971 in the light grey scheme used for non-combat rescue operations

Bottom right HC-130 crews of the Military Airlift Command and its reserve components are trained by the 1551st Flying Training Squadron, 1550th Combat Crew Training Wing at Kirtland AFB, New Mexico. Among the six Hercules (three HC-130H and three HC-130P) assigned to the 1551st FTS in the spring of 1989 was the last HC-130P built by Lockheed (66-0225). It is seen here taxiing on 27 April 1989 when it was fitted with engine nacelles borrowed from another aircraft

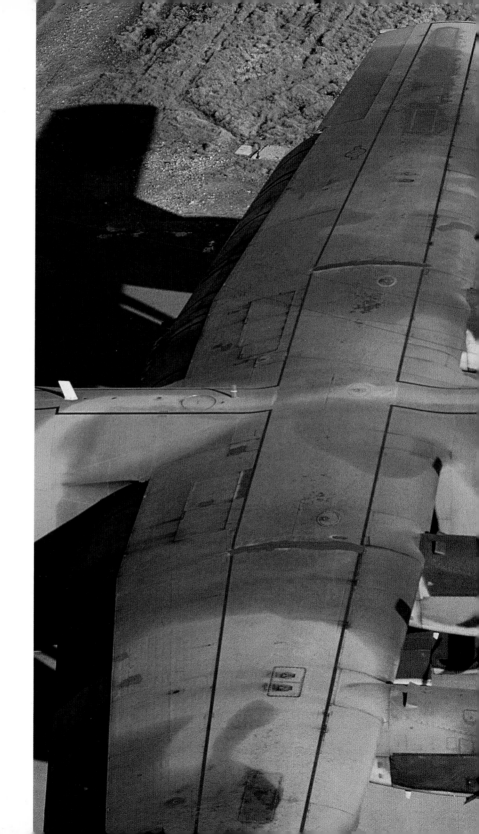

HC-130P (65-0991) of the 55th
ARRS at McClellan AFB on 1
February 1982

An HC-130H of the 71st ARRS displays his high-visibility SAR markings on the transient ramp at McClellan AFB on 22 January 1980

Below Close-up of the distinctive proboscis of an MC-130E equipped with Fulton STAR (Surface-to-Air-Recovery) yoke. This aircraft is on strength with the 7th Special Operations Squadron which, although based at Rhein-Main AB in Germany, is attached to the 1st Special Operations Wing at Eglin AFB, Florida

Right After making their first five jumps at the Army Airborne School, Fort Bragg, North Carolina, newly selected pararescue jumpers receive specialized training from instructors of the 1550th CCTW at Kirtland AFB and make day and night qualification jumps. Two young PJ trainees carefully check each other's equipment in the true-and-tested buddy method which they will use throughout their career whether making training or actual rescue jumps

Left An MC-130H *Combat Talon II* undergoing extreme cold weather testing at Eglin AFB in March 1969. Florida seems to be a strange place for the USAF to locate the climatic hangar in which to undertake cold weather testing! (*USAF*)

Above AC-130E of the 16th SOS, 8th TFW, at McClellan AFB on 13 July 1974. The aircraft carries an SUU-42 Flare Ejector Pods beneath its starboard wing. Ten months later *Spectres* from this unit played an important part during the rescue of the crew of the SS *Mayaguez* from Koh Tang Island off the coast of Cambodia

Below Landing at Pope AFB in June 1983, this AC-130H of the 16th SOS shows well the plexiglass observation bubble occasionally fitted beneath the aft loading ramp *(Paul Minert)*

Right *Night Stalker*, an AC-130A of the 711th SOS, 919th SOG, AFRES, at Rancho Murietta, California, during an air show in May 1988. The radome for the *Black Crow* system, the LLLTV/Laser rangefinder platform mounted in the doorway, one of the 20-mm Vulcan guns, and the infrared detector (on the right edge of the photo) are clearly visible. The photograph above, taken one year later, shows the *Spectre* emblem after it had been painted in full colours

Flying at dusk over the Gulf of
Mexico, this AC-130H of the 16th
SOS, 1st SOW, shows from fore to
aft the protruding barrels of its two
20-mm cannon, its 40-mm cannon
and its 105-mm howitzer (*USAF*)

Top The 304th AARS, 939th ARRG, AFRES, at the Portland International Airport is equipped with five HH-1Hs, one CH-3E, three HH-3Es, and six HC-130Hs (*Christian Jacquet-Francillon*)

Above Det 24 of the 40th ARRS provides support for the USAF Survival School at Fairchild AFB, Washington, with four HH-1Ns (*Christian Jacquet-Francillon*)

Right A new rescue pilot struggles to engage the probe of his Jolly Green in the starboard basket of an HC-130P of the 1551st FTS during a training sortie over the Rio Grande River near Albuquerque, New Mexico, on 28 April 1989

Below Previously operated by the 601st Tactical Air Control Wing at Sembach AB, Germany, as an HH-53B, this Super Jolly Green (70-01630) has been modified as an MH-53J and is now operated by the 20th SOS at Hurlburt Field, Florida (*USAF*)

Right The newest addition to the rotary wing fleet of the 1st SOW is the MH-60G Pave Hawk. More are on order to replace the HH-3Es still operated by AFRES and ANG rescue units(*USAF*)

To supplement its CH/
HH-3Es, HH-53Bs, CH/HH-53Cs,
and MH-60Gs in its training
program, the 1150th FTS has added
some ex-Marine Corps CH-53As,
including this Sea Stallion seen at
Kirtland AFB on 27 April 1972

To provide fire support during
combat rescue or commando
operations, the MH-53Hs and
MH-53Js are armed with Miniguns
on side hatches and an 0.50-in gun
on the aft ramp (*USAF*)

A crew chief from the 1st SOW
manning the port GAU-2B/A
Minigun of a Pave Hawk (*USAF*)

An MH-60G refuelling from the starboard tank of an HC-130P. A second Pave Hawk of the 1st SOW is flying in trail, ready to take on fuel from the Herk during a training sortie from Hurlburt Field. As is standard procedure during air-to-air refuelling the parachute doors on the aft fuselage of the HC-130 are open to enable the loadmaster to monitor the operation and warn the helicopter pilot if he should come too close (*USAF*)

A Pave Hawk kicks up dust while
flying over a Floridan training field
strewn with abandoned vehicles
(*USAF*)

Logair & CRAF

Left To supplement MAC's assets, LOGAIR contracts are placed with several carriers to transport spare parts and supplies, including ammunition, between Air Force Logistics Command bases and operational bases. This DC-9 of Evergreen International is seen landing at Nellis AFB, Nevada, on 20 August 1987

Below In the late seventies and early eighties Transamerica was one of the main contract carriers supplementing MAC. This Lockheed L-100-30 was photographed at Travis AFB on 2 July 1981

Donna Jean, a Lockheed Electra of Cam Air International, takes off at McClellan, the site of the Sacramento Air Logistics Center, at the start of a LOGAIR flight on 18 May 1985

In time of national emergency, the C-9As of the 375th Aeromedical Airlift Wing would be supplemented by McDonnell Douglas DC-9-80s (MD-80s) and Boeing 757s, such as this aircraft from America West Airlines

467258